Our Dad Bought a Mountain Bike

Stewart Williams

Text © 2021 by Stewart Williams
Illustrations copyright © 2021 by Stewart Williams

All rights reserved. No part of this book may be reproduced or transmitted in any form or by any means, electronic or mechanical, including photocopying, recording, or by any information storage or retrieval system without written permission of Stewart Williams.

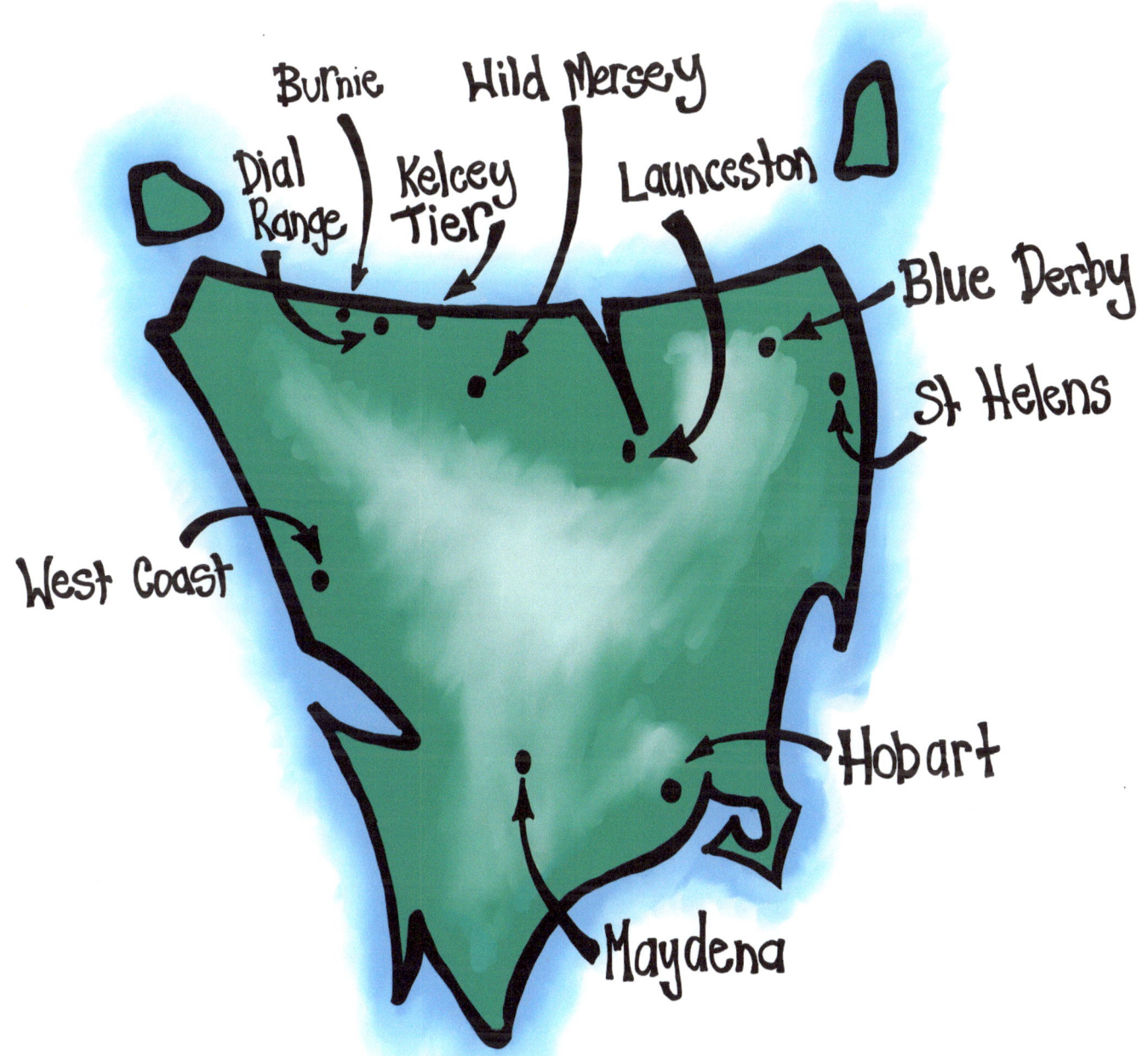

It started out just fine,
with rides along the park.
We'd stop to feed the ducks,
and be home before dark.

When Mum and Dad went out,
Dad would quickly find a mate,
they'd talk about bike riding,
yes... even on a date.[1]

Bikes... bikes... bikes...

[1] The author does not encourage nor endorse men talking to other men about mountain biking whilst on dates with their wives.

When Dad rode he'd check his phone
to see who he was beating.
"He must have used an e-bike," he'd say,
"and that's as good as cheating."[1]

[1] E-bikes are NOT cheating. They are great. The author wishes he had one.

"Shame on you," Dad said,
"to say such crazy things.
I was born to ride down mountains,
and besides... I'm allergic to bee stings."

Each day that Dad came home
he seemed to have less skin.
"I left some on the track," he'd say,
"for animals to live in."

Mum was buying band-aids every second day.
So then she bought some pads to make the 'hurties' go away.

Dad put on his new gear
to save his ageing skin.
"I'll be okay now," he said,
as he drove off with a grin.

They took Dad to the hospital
and he said (between his groans),
"My pads saved my skin today,
but didn't save my bones."

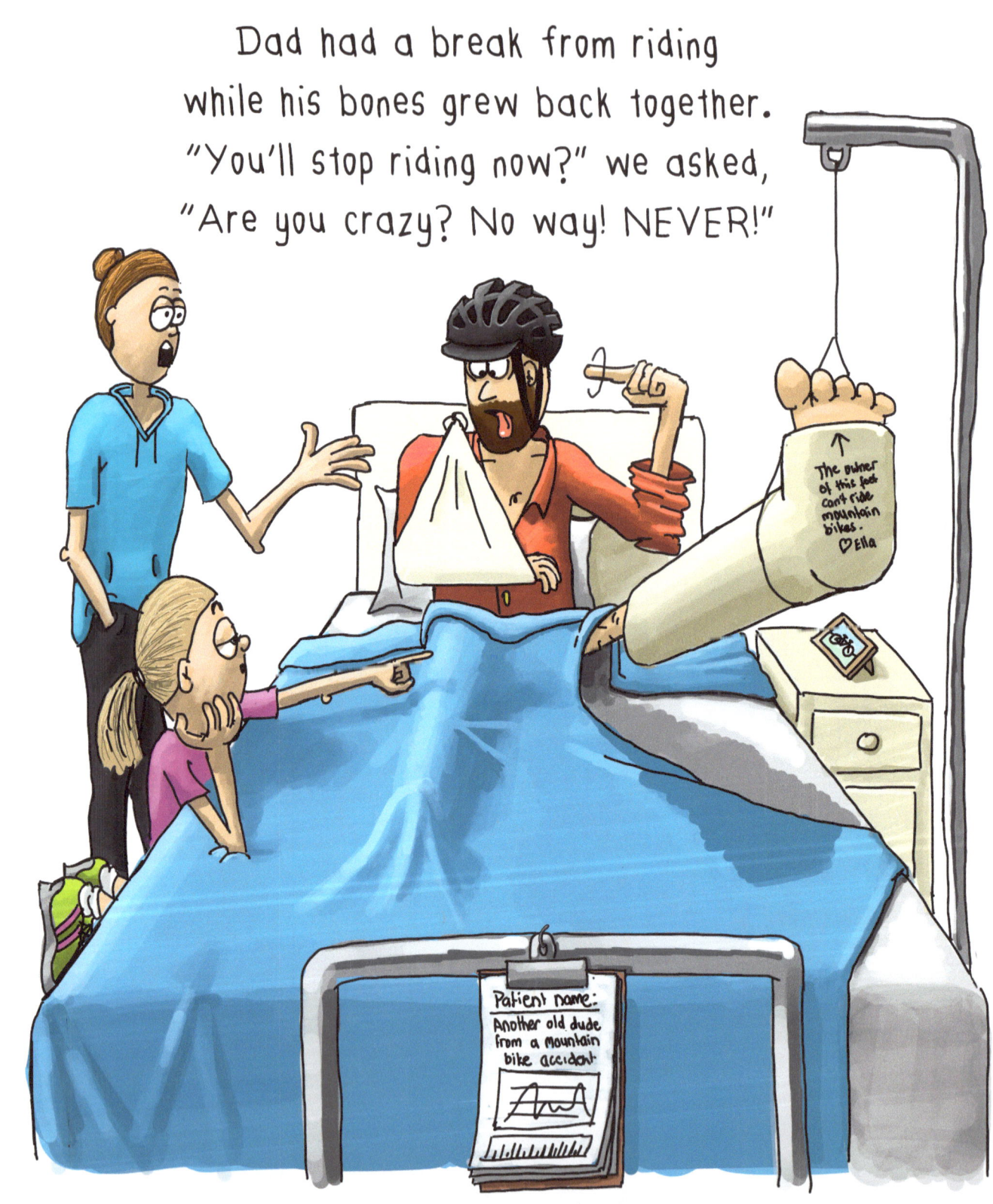

"I need a better bike," said Dad,
"as that's what caused my crash."
"Well, get a second job," Mum said,
"and buy one with that cash."

So Dad saved all his money and bought a brand new bike.

We thought he looked a little weird,
he thought he looked quite tough.

He'd travel around Tasmania
with his riding friends in tow.
Wild Mersey, Derby, Maydena and Penguin
are places he would go.

He'd send us photos of his trips,
and the places he would stay.
As soon as he got home,
he'd plan his next trip away.

Dad finally got *us* mountain bikes and took us to the track.

So Dad was quite surprised when we passed him halfway down.

Dad sulked for just a little while, and tried not to cry too loud.

More Titles By Stewart Williams

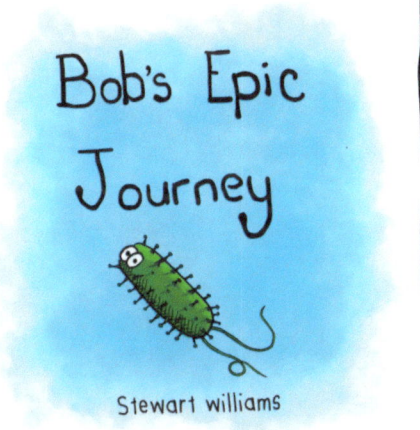

Contact / follow me on...

- Stewart Williams – Author / Illustrator
- stewart_williams_author
- Stewwriter@outlook.com

I'd love to hear from you.

www.ingramcontent.com/pod-product-compliance
Lightning Source LLC
Chambersburg PA
CBHW041431010526
44107CB00046B/1567